ENDOR‹ _____

"Paul's Big Letter is a gospel treasure chest for families. J. A. White breaks the book of Romans up into easy-to-understand chunks and uses kid-friendly language to communicate the key truths of the gospel found in the book of Romans. Grab a copy and take your family on a journey through Paul's most powerful letter, expecting the power of the gospel to affect your children."

Marty Machowski, Family Pastor and author of *Wonderfull: Ancient Psalms Ever New*, *The Ology*, *The Gospel Story Bible* and curriculum, *Long Story Short*, and other gospel resources for churches and families

"It is arguable that the Book of Romans contains the clearest, most complete, and most organized presentation of the Christian gospel anywhere to be found in the Bible. How important it is for Christians, young and old, to come to a fuller understanding of the glorious truths Paul presents here. Aaron White has written a short, clear, and easily-understandable overview of this Book that masterfully walks parents and children through Romans, highlighting what is most important to grasp and apply along the way. What a wonderful tool this is for discipling our children as well as for use in church, home-school, and Christian school curricula. I gladly commend this book and pray many will benefit from it."

Bruce A. Ware Professor of Christian Theology, Southern Seminary, Louisville, KY

"Romans is such a beautifully deep theological book of Scripture that it can be difficult to teach to our children. *Paul's Big Letter* does a fantastic job of breaking Romans down into points that can be easily digested. It contains a Biblically sound Gospel presentation, as well as real-life applications. It is well written, with questions and thoughtful consideration at the end of each chapter that makes for a delightful teaching tool!"

Lauren Hereford, Host, Tulips & Honey

A Kid-Friendly Journey Through Romans

J. Aaron White

H&E Kids, Peterborough, Ontario, Canada

This book is dedicated to those who long for little ones to see and savor the glory of the gospel of God (Rom. 1:1).

TABLE OF CONTENTS

INTRODUCTION

If you are reading this section of the book, you are likely a parent, grandparent, pastor, Sunday school teacher, or someone who simply cares a great deal about the spiritual formation of children. Whatever the case, I am thankful that you are burdened to see little ones grow into the "measure of the stature of the fullness of Christ" (Eph. 4:13). I want you to know from the outset that this resource was written by a sinner saved by grace who is blessed to be the husband of one amazing wife, the father of five wonderful children, and the pastor of a beloved church. Like you, I am concerned about the spiritual health of my children and want them to see and savor Christ in all of Scripture. As a preacher who spends a great deal of time in Paul's epistles, I found myself looking for resources for children ages 8–12 that would help them engage with these letters that make up the majority of the New Testament. After fruitless searches, I decided to create my own. I am guessing you have some questions, so let me see if I can beat you to the punch: *Why should children ages 8–12 study Paul's letters?* Aside from the sheer volume of content that comes to us from the apostle Paul, the doctrinal content of his epistles is meat and potatoes that our little ones need in their spiritual diet! Story Bibles, character studies, and picture books for children are a great blessing from the Lord for the nourishment of our children. However, they also need to engage with the mind-blowing truths that Paul sets forth.

Is it only for children ages 8–12? No, of course not. However, the content was created with this general age group in mind. If your little one is able to follow along and gain spiritual benefit from the study even though they are younger, great! Likewise, if older children find it helpful, that is cause for rejoicing as well. Ages 8–12 is merely a recommendation!

How do I use this study? There is one chapter for each chapter of Paul's epistle with each concluding with the *Big Idea* (what is the chapter about in one sentence), *Talk About It* (questions to probe the heart), and a *Key Verse* (one verse from the chapter to memorize). You may find that your little learners benefit from reading one chapter and spending a few days thinking through the questions, referring back to Paul's letter, and memorizing the *Key Verse*. Perhaps you find that tackling one chapter a day is helpful for your children. Also, this resource can be used for children's curriculum. However you choose to implement it, the main goal is for the kids to grasp what Paul is saying.

As I was developing the content for this study, I had my eleven-year-old daughter read it and make notes as to words she couldn't understand and concepts that were blurry. She made recommendations for changes that kids would appreciate. In short, this resource has been kid-approved, thus making it kid- friendly!

1

GOOD NEWS FOR BAD PEOPLE

Have you ever had a secret that you really, really, really wanted to tell someone? I'm not talking about a little secret like you're getting ice cream after lunch. I mean a big, awesome, life-altering, mind-boggling secret that is so huge you could barely stand it? That's exactly how the apostle Paul felt when he wrote to the Christians in Rome. Do you know where Rome is? That's right, it's in Italy (the country that looks like a boot). Paul wrote his letter around the year A.D. 57 while he was on his third big missionary journey and this is what he said: **"...I am eager to preach the gospel to you also who are in Rome. For I am not ashamed of the gospel, for it is the power of God for salvation to everyone who believes, to the Jew first and also to the Greek"** (Rom. 1:15–16).

Paul's *secret* was better than after-lunch ice cream, it was the good news of the gospel! So, what is the gospel and why is it good news? Great questions! Let me explain it by asking another question: Do you like to go outside on a clear night and look up at the stars? Do you think they would twinkle as brightly if the night sky were bright green or yellow? Of course not! The pitch black sky makes the stars more beautiful. This is the idea behind Paul's words in Romans chapter one: **"For the wrath of God is revealed from heaven against all ungodliness and unrighteousness of men, who by their unrighteousness suppress the truth"** (Rom. 1:18). Paul tells us the painful, awful truth about ourselves—we are *all* rebellious sinners who deserve God's wrath in hell! No matter where we live or who we are, the Bible says we're all bad people. You don't believe me? Listen to how Paul describes us: **"They were filled with all manner of unrigh-**

teousness, evil, covetousness, malice. They are full of envy, murder, strife, deceit, maliciousness,. They are gossips, slanderers, haters of God, insolent, haughty, boastful, inventors of evil, disobedient to parents, foolish, faithless, heartless, ruthless" (Rom. 1:29–31).** Although we do nice things like make our beds (sometimes) and say nice things (sometimes), our hearts are in rebellion against the loving God who made us. This is the black sky that we talked about. So, what about the stars?

Paul's good news is really, really, really good news when we understand how bad we really are. It's like hearing the doctor say that you have a bad disease; the news makes you sad. Then, the doctor smiles and tells you that he has the perfect cure; this news makes you happy! This is the good news that Paul wants to explain: **"For in it [the gospel] the righteousness of God is revealed from faith for faith, as it is written, 'The righteous shall live by faith'" (Rom. 1:17).** Although he won't give us all the details until chapter three (don't peak ahead!), Paul is telling us something amazing. Paul is telling us that God has done something that can make unrighteous (bad, sinful) people righteous (clean, forgiven). Not only that, he tells us that this salvation is all by *faith*! That means we don't have to earn our way to heaven; God reveals how this happens in the gospel, the good (awesome, amazing, God-glorifying, joy-giving) news.

Big Idea: We are sinful to the core but the good news of the gospel tells us how, by faith, we can be made righteous in the sight of a holy God.

Talk About It: Why would Paul say that we are all bad people if we do some nice things from time to time? How does hearing the bad news make the good news even better? What is the difference between having faith in something versus working to get something?

Key Verse: *"For I am not ashamed of the gospel, for it is the power of God for salvation to everyone who believes, to the Jew first and also to the Greek" (Rom. 1:16).*

2

THE PERFECT JUDGE . . . YIKES!

Justin could hear his mother raising her voice at his brother, Brad. "I can't believe you would throw that ball at my kitchen window after I've told you a hundred times not to!" said their mother. Justin really did feel sorry for Brad but he was also very happy that he wasn't the one who threw the baseball! But then it happened. As if she had some kind of superpower, Justin's mother yelled up the stairs in the direction where he was hiding and said,

"Justin, you better not be smiling right now!" How did she know he was smiling? Moms are amazing.

Paul had a similar situation with the church in Rome. After describing how sinful the non-Jewish world is in chapter one, he begins chapter two by addressing his Jewish friends: **"Therefore you have no excuse, O man, every one of you who judges. For in passing judgment on another you condemn yourself, because you, the judge, practice the very same things" (Rom. 2:1).** You see, Paul knew his Jewish friends were listening in (like Justin listened in while Brad was being punished). Paul also knew that they were probably getting a little self-righteous and were maybe even smiling! Do you know what *self-righteous* means? It's a way to describe someone who thinks they are better than everyone else or someone who thinks they are just fine the way they are. In Romans chapter two, Paul wants to show us that being born in a certain country, having a certain skin color, or doing good things isn't enough to save us from God's anger at our sin.

Paul wants us all to see that God is a perfect judge. A judge is the man or woman who wears a long black robe and makes important decisions in court cases. Since we have all broken God's law, we will all have to stand before him in his court one day. Here's the problem: God is a good and perfect judge who always does the right thing. That means he is always right to punish sinners—yikes! This is what Paul means when he says: **"For God shows no partiality" (Rom. 2:11).** God won't judge you because you are Jewish, white, black, rich, poor, or famous. The only thing that matters is if you are trusting in Jesus to take away your sins.

So, let's go back to our story about Justin and Brad. Even though Brad was wrong for throwing the ball through the window, Justin should never have laughed at him since he certainly had his own sin too! This is Paul's point in Romans chapter two. Paul wants Justin, Brad, you, and me to understand that we are *all* sinners who need a Savior. We should never trust anything other than Jesus to save us from God's righteous judgment. Paul tells us what is necessary to be saved from God's judgment of our sin: **"But a Jew is one inwardly, and circumcision is a matter of the heart, by the Spirit, not by the letter. His praise is not from man but from God" (Rom. 2:29).** Circumcision was the way that the Jewish people identified themselves as God's special people in the Old Testament. But Paul was warning them that just doing things on the outside without a change on the inside will not save us from God's justice. We need new hearts! So, let's stop laughing at other sinners and ask God to give us hearts that love and obey him.

Big Idea: Regardless of who we are or where we are from, we are all sinners in need of a Savior.

Talk About It: Have you ever laughed when someone else (i.e. your brother or sister, a friend, etc.) got in trouble? Why? How does Paul's words in Romans chapter two help you understand why you shouldn't make fun of other people when they sin?

Key Verse: *"For God shows no partiality" (Rom. 2:11).*

3

JESUS IS THE ANSWER

Think of your favorite superhero. Got it? Now, imagine him smashing through a brick wall and catching two thieves who are in the act of blowing up the bank vault! With ease, the villains are captured and handed over to the police. But then, your superhero's face changes. He notices that one of the bad guys is his nephew! With tears in his eyes, he runs over to the police, breaks the handcuffs off the young man, and says, "This is my dear nephew. I know he has broken the law, but I love him so much

I am going to set him free!" Does this seem ok to you? Is this really something the superhero should do? If you agree that he should, you've got a great, big, humongous theological question to answer!

Remember King David? We learned that God is a perfect judge, so how can a holy God let a murderer like David continue to live? Even crazier than that—how can a holy God show love to a sinner like David? Think about it. If David is a murderer and God is perfect, he shouldn't receive love, he should go to jail like the bank robber. But in the Bible we learn that God continued to love and care for David after he repented of his sin (Ps. 51). That seems nice, but David's sin still needs to be punished. Think of it this way—even if the bank robbers give the money they stole back to the bank, they still need to go to jail for their crimes, right? So, who is going to pay for David's crimes against God? If God just lets David off the hook, then God is no longer doing the right thing! This is a huge problem.

This is why Romans 3:21–26 is one of the most important parts of the Bible! How can unrighteous sinners like us become righteous? Listen to Paul:

"But now the righteousness of God has been manifested apart from the law, although the Law and the Prophets bear witness to it—the righteousness of God through faith in Jesus Christ for all who believe" (Rom. 3:21–22). Paul is telling us that the very God who should judge us offers us free forgiveness by trusting in his Son, Jesus Christ! No wrath, no hell. This is amazing; this is stupendous! But wait, there's still a problem. How are our sins punished? Where do they go? If they are not punished, then God is like the superhero who sweeps his nephew's sins under the rug!

This is why Paul's words are so important. The great apostle tells us how God can forgive sinners, make them righteous, and still be a good and perfect judge himself: **"It [the cross of Jesus] was to show his righteousness at the present time, so that he might be just and the justifier of the one who has faith in Jesus" (Rom. 3:26).** God can be just (the perfect judge) and justify (pardon, forgive) sinners because of the big, fancy word Paul used in verse 25: *propitiation*. Whoa! What does that word mean? It is a wrath-absorbing sacrifice. On the cross, Jesus took God's wrath for our sins and satisfied God's justice. So, when we repent of our sins and trust in Jesus, God knows that our sins were actually dealt with—by Jesus! So, how can a perfect judge forgive sinners? His perfect Son suffered their penalty. Jesus is the answer.

Big Idea: God can forgive sinners and still be perfect since his Son, Jesus Christ, suffered for their sin.

Talk About It: In your own words, explain why it is not ok to sweep sins under the rug. Why must sin be dealt with? Why can't you suffer for your own sin?

Key Verse: *"For all have sinned and fall short of the glory of God, and are justified by his grace as a gift, through the redemption that is in Christ Jesus"* *(Rom. 3:23–24).*

4

LIKE FATHER, LIKE SONS

Imagine this: A man comes to your family's home, knocks on the door, and asks if he can tell an amazing story. Would you listen to him? The man looks a little funny, but he seems nice and very sincere about what he wants to tell your family. Your dad nervously invites him in and offers him a cup of coffee. The man then begins to tell a story about how your family's great, great, great, great ancestors were aliens from Mars. "Your relatives were nine feet tall with big ears and bright blue skin," the man says. Your father looks angry; your mom looks nervous. Even though the man is kind, your father eventually asks him to leave your house. Once he leaves, your dad closes the door and says, "That was the weirdest thing I have ever heard!"

For many of Paul's Jewish friends, his message (the gospel of Jesus Christ) seemed like a strange story. However, Paul desperately wanted his friends to understand that his gospel was the same message in the Old Testament that they studied. In order to prove it to them, Paul needed to show them that their great, great, great, great ancestor believed the same message that he preached. Paul wasn't talking about blue aliens from Mars; he was talking about Abraham! The Jews loved Abraham but they made a wrong assumption—they thought Abraham was saved because of his good works. Paul wanted everyone in Rome to understand that even Abraham was saved by grace through faith in God's promise of salvation, not by trying to be good.

Here is what Paul said: **"For what does the Scripture say? 'Abraham believed God, and it was counted to him as righteousness'" (Rom. 4:3).** Paul is referring to Genesis 15:6 (way back in the beginning of the Bible). In Genesis, Abram (his name eventually became Abraham) trusted that God was willing and able to keep his promises. He didn't work for it; he didn't have to prove anything to God. Paul wanted his friends in Rome to understand that Abraham was saved by faith in God's promise to save. This is the heart of Paul's message: sinners are saved by trusting in God's mercy and grace, not by trying to win God's approval. Paul says, **"And to the one who does *not* work but believes in him who justifies the ungodly, his faith is counted as righteousness" (Rom. 4:5, emphasis added).** This is great news! Sinners like us are saved in the same way Abraham was saved–by faith in God alone!

Even though Paul's message sounded like a story from Mars, his friends should have seen that it was the same message that the entire Old Testament taught! There's even a cool word in Paul's argument: *counted*. Paul is not talking about math, so relax. He says that when Abraham (or anyone else) stops trying to earn God's favor and simply trusts him in faith, God considers them to be righteous even though, on the inside, they are not. Abraham lived a long time before Jesus came to earth but he looked forward in faith to the day that his sins would be dealt with. For us, we live a long time after Jesus died on the cross so we look backwards and trust that his sacrifice for our sins satisfied God's justice. Like Abraham, we must trust God's gracious promise to forgive us and count us as righteous. This is not a crazy story about aliens, this is the gospel truth.

Big Idea: Like Abraham, we are considered to be righteous by trusting in God's promises.

Talk About It: In what way(s) do you trust your good works to earn favor with God? Why won't your good deeds ever be enough? What does it mean to trust or put your faith in something?

Key Verse: *"And to the one who does not work but believes in him who justifies the ungodly, his faith is counted as righteousness" (Rom. 4:5).*

5

THE ULTIMATE ADAM

It's the last half of a very important soccer game for your team. You've worked hard all season practicing passing and shooting; you are ready to rock! Your team is down by two goals, but everyone seems ready to get back in the game and push for the win. The whistle blows and the forward players clash and battle for possession of the poor black and white ball that's taking a pummeling. Finally, the ball flies in the direction of your opponent's goal—run! As you and your teammates charge toward certain victory, you hear the referee blow his whistle and the players slow down to a jog and finally stop. What happened? With a frightful look on your face, you realize that one of your players committed a foul and now you've lost possession of the ball. One simple mistake has placed your opponents in a position to maintain their lead. Sure enough. Your team tries but it never regains the momentum it had before the fateful foul. You lose. It hurts.

When one player on a team breaks the rules, the entire team suffers for it. Although you don't commit the foul, the person who did is wearing the same uniform as you which means you get penalized too. This is exactly what happened with our distant relative, Adam: **"Therefore, just as sin came into the world through one man, and death through sin, and so death spread to all men because all sinned" (Rom. 5:12).** As humans, Adam was our team captain (sort of). He committed a major foul in the Garden of Eden and we all got penalized as his fellow humans. Like the kid on your soccer team who lost the game for his teammates, Adam lost the biggest game of all for his entire team — the human race!

Just in case you're getting angry at Adam, go back and read Paul's words again: **"death spread to all men because all sinned" (5:12).** Not only are we guilty by association with Adam's sin, we also have our own sins that make us guilty. Even though Adam cost us the ball, we've all committed personal fouls in our time on the field too! Sinners like you and I need a better team and a better team captain. Actually, we need a perfect team captain! This is where Romans chapter five brings us great news: **"For as by the one man's disobedience the many were made sinners, so by the one man's obedience the many will be made righteous" (Rom. 5:19).** It might sound a little funny, but Jesus is the ultimate Adam.

Let's look at the stats for each captain. Adam disobeyed God, failed to love and worship God, and did not protect his wife (Gen. 3:1–8). Jesus, on the other hand, always loved, obeyed, and glorified his Father, never sinned, and saved his sinful bride (i.e. all those who trust him as their Lord and Savior) by dying in her place for her sins (1 Pet. 1:17–19). Jesus has a perfect record—no fouls! If we are on Jesus' team, we don't have any fouls either. This is why

Paul wants his Roman friends as well as all of us to see that Jesus is the ultimate Adam. If we turn from our sin and put our trust in him, his perfect record is given to us. This is amazing news! So, who is your captain?

Big Idea: Instead of inheriting death and judgment in Adam, we inherit life and peace by faith in Christ Jesus.

Talk About It: Have you ever been in trouble for something someone else did? How did it make you feel? What fouls (sins) have you committed yourself that need to be forgiven? In your own words, explain how Jesus is the ultimate Adam.

Key Verse: *"For as by the one man's disobedience the many were made sinners, so by the one man's obedience the many will be made righteous"* (Rom. 5:19).

6

WE HAVE A NEW MASTER

You may be saying, "How can I have a *new* master? I didn't think I had an old one!" Think about it, you go outside and play, eat peanut butter and jelly sandwiches, and ride your bike without someone in a uniform telling you what to do every five minutes, right? So, what *master* do you have? Brace yourself, what you're about to read might sound weird. Your master's name is sin. As a matter of fact, everyone has the same master; you're not alone. Listen to the apostle Paul in Romans chapter six: **"Do you not know that if you present your-selves to anyone as obedient slaves, you are slaves of the one whom you obey, either of sin, which leads to death, or of obedience, which leads to righteousness?"** (Rom. 6:16).

Here is what Paul is saying: the way you act shows which master you serve, either sin or God. Remember when we learned about Adam? Ever since the Fall in Genesis chapter three, we have all been born as slaves of sin. This means that although we might do some nice things such as helping our brothers or sisters, obeying our parents, or finishing our homework, we do not love God with all our hearts and do not consistently obey him with joy. Listen to the way Paul describes humans who are in bondage to sin: **"For we ourselves were once foolish, disobedient, led astray, slaves to various passions and pleasures, passing our days in malice and envy, hated by others and hating one another"** (Titus 3:3). Everyone, even Paul, comes into the world with a heart that favors sin over God! Sin tells us what to do and we obey. Paul is encouraging us to live as people who have been given a new (and way better) master.

This is the good news of the gospel: **"But thanks be to God, that you who were once slaves of sin have become obedient from the heart to the standard of teaching to which you were committed, and, having been set free from sin, have become slaves of righteousness" (Rom. 6:17–18).** By God's amazing grace, sinners who trust in Jesus to forgive their sins are unshackled from their former master, sin, and given a new master, the Lord Jesus Christ. How is Jesus a better master than sin? That's a great question!

Let's look at the differences between our masters: sin tempts us to do things that make us ashamed (Rom. 6:21) but Jesus takes away our shame and gives us joy (2 Cor. 5:21). Sin separates us from God and the joy of his presence (Isa. 59:1–2) but Jesus brings us into God's presence where we experience joy (Ps. 16:11; 1 Pet. 3:18). When Jesus is our master, we are no longer slaves to joy-killing sin. Our new master is working all the time for our greatest joy by setting us free from sin and giving us greater and greater appetites for joy in God. Our old master, sin, was always telling us to do things that only ended in shame, hurt, and further distance from God. Our new master, Jesus, is always working for

our good, bringing us into God's presence, and of-
fering us true joy. By faith in Christ, we have a new
master.

Big Idea: By God's amazing grace, we are set free from our old master (sin) and given a new and better master (Jesus Christ).

Talk About It: What does it mean to be a slave to sin? In your own words, explain how the way we live our lives and the things we really love (and find pleasure in) show who our master is? When Jesus is our master, does it mean we don't sin anymore? Why or why not?

Key Verse: *"But thanks be to God, that you who were once slaves of sin have become obedient from the heart to the standard of teaching to which you were committed" (Rom. 6:17).*

7

GOOD LAW, BAD HEARTS

Do you ever get tired of the bad guy in your favorite cartoon or show? Every time there's a nice day with sunshine and blue skies, he always seems to find a way to make trouble. Picture this scene: A long, winding highway curves its way through the countryside on a beautiful autumn day. The trees are neon red, yellow, and orange. Up ahead is a white sign that clearly states that the speed limit is fifty-five miles per hour. If the story ended here, we could all sleep well. But wait, there's more. The bad guy has been hiding in the backseat the entire time! With green teeth and evil eyes, he leans forward and begins to whisper in the driver's ear. He hisses, "That's too slow, you should be able to go a lot faster. You're a safe driver, go ahead and press the gas pedal." His advice seems to make sense, so the driver obeys. His speedometer inches from fifty-five to ninety miles per hour! As the engine roars under the hood, he approaches a sharp turn in the road. The driver panics and stomps on the brake but—too late. His car spins out of control, flies off the road, and is turned into a ghastly pile of metal and rubber. What happened? Was it the speed limit's fault? No, of course not. The bad guy was sin and the driver's evil heart loved what he had to say.

This is a picture of what Paul wants his readers to understand in Romans chapter seven. In short, he needs to explain what he said in the previous chapter: **"For sin will have no dominion over you, since you are not under law but under grace" (Rom. 6:14).** *Not under God's law?* Does that mean we can sin without consequences? Is the law a bad thing? These were some of the questions that Paul needed to answer. First, Paul tells us what happens when a good law comes into contact with a stony heart: **"What then shall we say? That the law is sin? By no means! Yet if it had not been for the law, I would not have known sin. For I would not have known what it is to covet if the law had not said, 'You shall not covet'" (Rom. 7:7).** Second, like the speed limit sign, Paul wants to show that sin uses God's good and perfect law as a weapon to enslave us: **"But sin, seizing an opportunity through the commandment, produced in me all kinds of covetousness. For apart from the law, sin lies dead. I was once alive apart from the law, but when the commandment came, sin came alive and I died" (Rom. 7:8–9).** Like the bad guy in our story, sin uses the law (which is good and holy) as a weapon against us.

Paul has already told us the truth about ourselves earlier in the Book of Romans: **"None is righteous, no, not one; no one understands; no one seeks for God" (Rom. 3:10–11).** When God's good law comes into contact with our bad hearts, sin comes alive. But don't get discouraged! The law of God convicts us of our sin and, by his grace, directs us to the only place where our sin can be cleansed: **"Wretched man that I am! Who will deliver me from this body of death? Thanks be to God through Jesus**

Christ our Lord" (Rom. 7:24–25). When God's good law convicts our bad hearts, the only place where we can find freedom and joy is in Jesus Christ and his cross.

Big Idea: Sin uses the good and perfect law of God to tempt our bad hearts to rebel.

Talk About It: Describe a time when you were tempted to break a rule at home, at school, or in town. Did you rebel against the rule? If so, why? What must happen inside of us to make us want to obey God's good laws?

Key Verse: *"For while we were living in the flesh, our sinful passions, aroused by the law, were at work in our members to bear fruit for death" (Rom. 7:5).*

8

PROMISES THAT GIVE US JOY

"Make way!" the soldier cried. Behind him were four large, armor-clad warriors carrying a stretcher with a man on it. The sweaty, bruised soldier was none other than their general. He had been on the battlefield for three days without rest since he refused to leave his men in the midst of the fight. Finally, he collapsed from exhaustion and was carried to a medical tent by his men. After sipping some cool water and having his wounds bandaged, he sat up and looked around at his beloved soldiers. "How goes the battle?" he asked in a gruff voice. His second officer smiled and replied, "Sir, the enemy is retreating and victory is near." The general sighed with relief as he leaned his sweaty head back against the wall. Through his chapped lips he muttered, "Praise God."

This scene is not from a movie; it is a representation of the Christian life. Coming out of Romans chapters six and seven, we feel weary in our battle against sin and we need to be assured that victory will indeed come. The apostle Paul is prepared to assure weary Christians with one of the most beautiful chapters in the Bible: Romans eight. In our fight against sin, we need to hear Paul's opening words: **"There is therefore now no condemnation for those who are in Christ Jesus" (Rom. 8:1).** Even though we struggle in this life, we do it with the knowledge that we are not under God's condemnation! That means we are not going to be judged for our sins since we are "in Christ Jesus." This is amazing news! This one verse is like a cup of cold water to a weary soldier. But Paul is not done.

For genuine Christians — those who fight their sin and trust in God's promise of salvation in Jesus —

we have a glorious future ahead. Since we have been adopted by God into his family, we can endure the pain of this life with joy: **"The Spirit himself bears witness with our spirit that we are children of God, and if children, then heirs—heirs of God and fellow heirs with Christ, provided we suffer with him in order that we may also be glorified with him" (Rom. 8:16–17).** In battle, we can count on being hurt. Like the weary general, every Christian gets bumps and bruises in this life as we fight sin. That's why Paul's words are so glorious: we are heirs with Christ. An heir is someone who inherits something that belongs to another person. Paul makes his point clearer a little later in Romans eight: **"He who did not spare his own Son but gave him up for us all, how will he not also with him graciously give us all things" (Rom. 8:32).** This does not mean that we will get all the toys and ice cream we want—those will only rot and go away. No, Paul is saying something much greater: we will enjoy eternal life with Jesus and see his glory (Jn. 17:24).

Weary soldiers need encouragement. For those who fight their sin and trust Jesus, Romans chapter eight is like a soft bed upon which we can rest. We know that everything in this life, good or bad, is working for our ultimate good (Rom. 8:28). We know that God chose us and that he will never let us go (Rom. 8:30). We know that nothing, even the worst of things, can separate us from God's love (Rom. 8:35–39). These are promises that give weary soldiers much joy.

Big Idea: God's grace empowers us to endure suffering in this life and to look forward to massive joy in the future.

Talk About It: How important is being encouraged when you're feeling weak? Why is it good news that "there is therefore now no condemnation for those who are in Christ Jesus"? How is it comforting to know that God is at work in every situation in our lives? What are Christians going to inherit in the future?

Key Verse: *"He who did not spare his own Son but gave him up for us all, how will he not also with him graciously give us all things?" (Rom. 8:32).*

58

9

WHAT IT MEANS TO BE KING

A man wearing a red and blue uniform respectfully approached the tall, golden throne upon which the king sat. Removing his hat, he bowed at the waist and said, "Your majesty, we have captured the two men who tried to harm you." Two weeks prior, a couple of men tried to clobber the king with wooden clubs when he came riding through the town square. Thankfully, the king's guards were able to stop them but they escaped into the crowd. Now, the criminals were shackled and awaiting their sentence from the king whom they tried to harm. The king's voice thundered through the halls of his courtroom as he exclaimed, "Bring them to me!" The other guards led the two men into the king's court and they stood with their heads down before the throne. The king pointed his scepter at the man on the right and motioned for him to be taken away to prison. Left alone, the other shook uncontrollably. The king said to the remaining criminal, "I would like you to serve in my court. I will let you eat at my table and perhaps you will grow to love the king you tried to destroy." Amazed, the man wept with joy.

You're probably thinking, "That's not fair!" Am I right? Why did the king send one man to prison and let the other man eat with him? Before we go too far, let's remember one important detail: they *both* deserved to go to prison (or worse). If the king were being fair, he would send them both to prison. The fact that he chose to show kindness to either of them is amazing! This is Paul's point in Romans chapter nine. God, the king of all creation, could have destroyed everyone since we are all sinners (go back and look at Romans 3:9–20). More specifically, some of the people who read Paul's letter may have wondered why all the Jews did not believe the gospel. Paul explains that salvation has never been because of someone's race or good works. God, the king, is the one who chooses whom to save: **"So then it depends not on human will or exertion, but on God, who has mercy" (Rom. 9:16).** Is God playing favorites? You might have a kid in your class who is really good at kickball and you show him favor over the other players to get him on your team. Thankfully, this is not how God does things. He chooses to show amazing mercy to really bad sinners simply because he is kind.

Paul uses another example that might help us. Have you ever tried to make anything out of clay? The easiest thing to make is probably a snake or a worm. However, if you don't like your snake, you can smash it and roll it into a ball. You can then form your ball of clay into a penguin, shark, or lion. You have control over the clay. This is what Paul says about God, the King: **"Has the potter no right over the clay, to make out of the same lump one vessel for honorable use and another for dishonorable use?" (Rom. 9:21).** So, here's the bottom line of Romans chapter nine: God is the holy creator of all things and he can do as he pleases. Thankfully, he is a kind and gracious king! Instead of throwing away the whole ball of clay because it's dirty, he chooses to save parts of it and make beautiful things from it. This is what it means to be king.

Big Idea: God is the holy creator and he does all things according to his good and righteous will.

Talk About It: Describe a time in your life when you said, "That's not fair!" How is this situation different from God choosing to save some (even many) of his rebellious people? How does the cross of Jesus Christ remind us that God is a good king?

Key Verse: *"So then he has mercy on whomever he wills, and he hardens whomever he wills" (Rom. 9:18).*

10

SPEAK UP!

What would you do if your best friend in the whole wide world was playing with a toy truck on railroad tracks? These aren't just any railroad tracks, they are busy tracks upon which dozens of huge trains come blasting through town every day! Would you slowly walk over to where he is playing, lazily cup your hands around your mouth, and quietly whisper for him to move? No way! If you're a good friend, you will sprint over to the tracks, cup your hands around your mouth, and scream,

"Geettttt oouuuttt ooofffff tthheee waaaayyyyy!!!!!!!
If your friend ignored you, you would probably
run over, grab him by the jacket, and pull with all
your might to get him off of the dangerous tracks.
Should it be any different when we see people who
are playing next to a cliff? What if hell were right
below the cliff? After telling us that God chooses
whom he will save, Paul amazingly tells us to
speak up!

Although God is the king who has control of the
clay, he chooses to use people in his work of salvation: **"For everyone who calls on the name of the
Lord will be saved" (Rom. 10:13).** Paul goes on to
answer his own dilemma: **"How then will they call
on him in whom they have not believed? And
how are they to believe in him of whom they have
never heard? And how are they to hear without
someone preaching?" (Rom. 10:14).** Do you see
how cool, amazing, and life-changing this is? The
king of the universe chooses to use little, sinful people like us for his purposes! It's not enough to want
other people to know, love, and serve the Lord Jesus Christ, we must speak up!

Let's go back and listen to Paul: **"And how are they to preach unless they are sent? As it is written, 'How beautiful are the feet of those who preach the good news!'" (Rom. 10:15).** Maybe your feet are dirty and stinky from playing outside, but if you tell the good news of the gospel to others, your feet are beautiful since they brought you to a needy sinner! Someone who pulls another person from the danger of an oncoming train has really beautiful feet.

In this book, we have said that sinners are saved by God's grace through faith in Jesus Christ. This is true. Now, listen to what Paul says in Romans ten: **"So faith comes from hearing, and hearing through the Word of Christ" (Rom. 10:17).** In other words, sinners need to *hear* the gospel. This means that we need to know the gospel and, by God's grace, go and tell the gospel to the world. Now, think about this: we enjoy talking about the things we love. So, if Jesus Christ is our Savior, Lord, and friend, we should enjoy talking about him. Do you have a best friend? Do you ever talk about him or her? I bet you do. Although it might be scary to share the gospel with other people, remember that you are talking about the Person who gives you the most joy. Also, remember that the message of the gospel is **"the power of God for salvation" (Rom. 1:16).** You might be a kid, but you have the most powerful message in the world. So, speak up!

Big Idea: God has chosen to save sinners through the preaching of the gospel of his Son, Jesus Christ.

Talk About It: Have you ever saved a friend or sibling from getting hurt? How did it make you feel? Are you nervous about sharing the gospel with others? How can Romans 1:16 help give you courage?

Key Verse: *"So faith comes from hearing, and hearing through the word of Christ" (Rom. 10:17).*

11

GOD ALWAYS KEEPS HIS WORD

Have you ever been waiting to get picked up after school, from a game, or from a friend's house and started wondering if your mom or dad had forgotten you? What a scary feeling! There you are all alone, straining to look as far down the road as possible for any hint of the sight of your parents' car. The minutes seem like hours and the sun seems to be sinking like a rock in a pond—oh no! "They said they'd be here at 5 o'clock," you mutter to yourself in disgust. Finally, you hear the familiar sound of your beloved family car (or van, truck, motorcycle, or go kart) coming down the road! You breathe a sigh of relief and are a tad bit embarrassed that you doubted your parents. In relief, you throw your backpack and soccer ball onto the seat and plop down with a smile.

Even though our human parents are often trustworthy, there is only one parent who perfectly keeps his word—God Almighty. Our moms and dads might actually forget to pick us up, but God never forgets anything he has promised and is always on time—always. This is Paul's point in Romans chapter eleven. At the very end of the previous chapter, Paul said this: **"But of Israel he says, 'All day long I have held out my hands to a disobedient and contrary people'" (Rom. 10:21).** Paul knows what some people will be thinking when they hear this: *Has God given up on Israel?* You see, in the Old Testament, God made a lot of promises to Israel. He said things like this: **"Remember these things, O Jacob, and Israel, for you are my servant; I formed you; you are my servant; O Israel, you will not be forgotten by me" (Isa. 44:21).** Even though many of Paul's fellow Jews rejected the gospel, he reminds us of God's purposes: **"So too at** the present time there is a remnant, chosen by grace" (Rom. 11:5). Has God forgotten to save the Jews he promised to save? No way, he will save the remnant (a set number of people chosen by God).

It's true, many of the Jewish people today still reject the gospel of Jesus Christ. However, there is a remnant that *will* be saved—by grace. This last point is important since we often get prideful when we think that God loves us more than someone else. Perhaps some of Paul's non-Jewish friends became arrogant when they learned that **"through their [Jews] trespass salvation has come to the Gentiles" (Rom. 11:11).** So, Paul makes sure to remind us that Jews and Gentiles are *both* saved by grace alone, a truth that should make us all humble and thankful.

Has God forgotten his Jewish remnant? Of course not. God's plan of salvation may be hard to understand at times, but we know that he will not fail to save all of his elect people—Jew and Gentile. Paul makes clear that we are all at God's mercy: **"For God has consigned all to disobedience, that he may have mercy on all" (Rom. 11:32).** This made Paul gush with amazement: **"Oh, the depth of the** riches and wisdom and knowledge of God! How unsearchable are his judgments and how inscrutable his ways!" **(Rom. 11:33).** Our amazing God always keeps his word.

Big Idea: God will save all of his elect chosen people, both Jew and Gentile.

Talk About It: In your own words, explain how the cross of Jesus Christ assures us that God always keeps his word (see also Romans 8:32). How should the knowledge that God has a remnant of people who *will* be saved encourage you to share the gospel? Why should knowing that we are all saved by grace alone make you humble?

Key Verse: *"Oh, the depth of the riches and wisdom and knowledge of God! How unsearchable are his judgments and how inscrutable his ways!" (Rom. 11:33).*

12

PUTTING OUR NEW HEARTS TO WORK

I remember the first (and only) time I went cliff diving. It was a hot summer day and some friends and family found a deep pond filled with cool, blue water. We found a ledge that was approximately forty feet high and were daring one another to jump into the water below. One by one, the adults sailed through the air with not-so-cool screams and screeches until they splashed and disappeared. With trembling legs, I slowly walked to the end of the ledge and stared down at my friends bobbing in the water. "Just plug your nose and you'll be fine! Jump!" they taunted. I stood on the ledge wrestling with my fear for at least ten minutes. All the while, my friends were reassuring me that jumping is not only fun but safe too. Finally, I lifted my right foot, plugged my nose, and leaned forward off the ledge. I felt like I was skydiving until I slammed into the water below. I popped up from the water's surface with a nervous smile—I survived!

When it comes to taking risks, most of us need some serious reassurance. The apostle Paul knew all about this and so he repeatedly offers encouragement, reassurance, and promises of joy before he calls Christians to do hard things. In Romans chapter twelve, Paul begins to tell us how we should live our lives as followers of Jesus. He calls on us to do some hard and risky things, but he always points us to the reassurance of the gospel: **"I appeal to you therefore, brothers, by the mercies of God, to present your bodies as a living sacrifice, holy and acceptable to God, which is your spiritual worship" (Rom. 12:1).** We need some serious reassurance! That's why Paul tells us to remember everything he has said in Romans so far: God sent his Son to die for unworthy sinners. Since we know that God is good, just, loving, holy, and extremely merciful, we can trust that giving our entire lives to him will be a good and joyful experience no matter what happens. We are motivated to live for his glory because he is merciful!

Paul goes on to tell us to do something really hard: be humble and honor other people (Rom. 12:3–8). Being humble and seeking to bless others does not come naturally to sinners like us. But because of God's mercy in Christ, Paul says: **"Let love be genuine. Abhor what is evil; hold fast to what is good. Love one another with brotherly affection. Outdo one another in showing honor" (Rom. 12:9–10).** Whoa! Paul wants us to work hard at making other people look good — that's hard! But wait, there's more: **"Bless those who persecute you; bless and do not curse them" (Rom. 12:14).** The only thing in the universe that can empower us to take these kinds of risks is the mercy of God. Jumping from a cliff is a piece of cake compared to giving our bodies, future plans, and comfort away for the sake of others. However, listen to the merciful words of Jesus: **"Truly, I say to you, there is no one who has left house or brothers or sisters or mother or father or children or lands, for my sake** and for the gospel, who will not receive a hundredfold now in this time, houses and brothers and sisters and mothers and children and lands, with persecutions, and in the age to come eternal life" (Mk. 10:29–30).

Big Idea: God's grace not only forgives our sins, it empowers us to live for his glory.

Talk About It: Have you ever needed reassurance to do something scary? What was it? What comforted you so that you could follow through? What has Paul said in chapters one through eleven that would offer us comfort and reassurance as we seek to live for God's glory?

Key Verse: *"I appeal to you therefore, brothers, by the mercies of God, to present your bodies as a living sacrifice, holy and acceptable to God, which is your spiritual worship" (Rom. 12:1).*

13

RESPECT THE BADGE, RESPECT YOUR NEIGHBOR

Natalie was terrified. One minute she was brushing her doll's hair while riding in the backseat of her family's minivan; the next minute she woke up to the sound of sirens. A red truck pulled out in front of their family's van and Natalie's dad couldn't stop in time. The van crashed into the truck, the airbags went off, glass went flying, and her dad stopped breathing. Thankfully a young police man named Luke was on patrol that day. Officer Luke sped to the scene of the accident, pulled Natalie's father out of the van and gave him the medical attention he needed. Natalie's dad started breathing again just as the ambulance arrived to take him and Natalie to the hospital. After their hospital visit, Natalie and her father met the young policeman who saved their lives and thanked him with tears.

Not only should Natalie and her father thank Luke, they should also thank God! The apostle Paul tells us that police officers are gifts from God to protect and serve us: **"Let every person be subject to the governing authorities. For there is no authority except from God, and those that exist have been instituted by God" (Rom. 13:1).** The reason Christians are to honor authorities (like police officers) is because God put them in that position. You might be thinking, "What a minute! What if an officer wants me to do something sinful? Do I still obey?" That's a great question and to answer it, let's quickly go back to the Old Testament. In Daniel chapter three, King Nebuchadnezzar made an idol of himself and demanded that everyone worship it. Although he was the king (the one with authority), Shadrach, Meshach, and Abednego knew it would be sinful to worship anything other than God. These three young men endured punishment instead of disobeying God (read about their amazing rescue in Daniel 3:8–30). There are times to disobey kings and officers quietly and humbly. However, Paul wants Christians to strive to honor and bless those whom God has placed in authority over them.

Paul also wants Christians to love other people: **"Love does no wrong to a neighbor; therefore love is the fulfilling of the law" (Rom. 13:10).** Every command in Scripture (no lying, no stealing, no murder) points back to this basic principle — love. If the grace of God has forgiven my sins and filled my heart with joy, I will look for ways to love and bless other people. If I am looking for ways to love and bless them, I won't kill them or steal their bike! Paul's words are simple yet amazing. Besides, if we love others the way God has loved us in Christ, the police officers will have an easier job!

Respecting authority and loving other people are not things that sinners naturally do. As we learned in Romans chapter one, we are all naturally rebellious and selfish. So how can Paul ask us to do such hard things? Here is his answer: **"But put on the Lord Jesus Christ, and make no provision for the flesh, to gratify its desires" (Rom. 13:14).** Some people put on uniforms and badges before they go outside. For Christians, we are to put on (trust, obey, love) the Lord Jesus Christ. This is how we can respect the badge and respect our neighbors.

Big Idea: Christians are to respect authorities (such as government officials and police officers) and love other people by the power of God's grace.

Talk About It: What are some ways that police officers bless other people? How can you bless police officers? When might it be alright to disobey someone in authority? If you have to disobey, what should be your attitude?

Key Verse: *"Love does no wrong to a neighbor; therefore love is the fulfilling of the law" (Rom. 13:10).*

... the ... Crude ... ... authority ...
such as government ... state ... police officers),
and law ... people by the powers that God's given

Talk About It: What are we ... ... that good ...
officers in ... these people? ... ... bless people officer ... ... might ... ... disable
some me in ... ... passes ... ...
about it ... world ... ...

Key Verse: "... we ... ... a multitude
... ... in the light ... ... Isaiah
9:16

14

GETTING TO KNOW OUR CONSCIENCES

Matthew and his buddies loved to play in the woods behind his house. On a mild October day, Matthew and his friends headed out into the forest. With shouts of joy and laughter, the boys ran as fast as they could through the thick underbrush. Each of them was racing to be the first one to arrive at their secret tree fort! Matthew's dad gave him some leftover boards and nails that he and his friends used to create their very own castle (well, at least it felt like a castle to them). Once the last boy arrived at the fort, they recited the secret password to-gether and went inside. That's when the trouble started. Joseph, one of Matthew's friends, pulled a lighter from his pocket and began lighting sticks and leaves on fire then blowing them out quickly. Although the other boys seemed to enjoy Joseph's tricks, Matthew felt something in his tummy. He knew that Joseph was not supposed to be playing with fire. How did Matthew know that what Joseph was doing was wrong? His conscience told him.

Our conscience is a gift from God; it's that little voice inside of us that tells us when something we are doing is wrong. Sometimes our conscience keeps us from sinning—great! Other times, our conscience gets confused as to what is sinful. Paul's friends in Rome loved Jesus and wanted to follow him. But for some of them, their consciences could not agree about what things were ok for them to do. In particular, they didn't agree on what they were allowed to eat. This might sound funny to you since you likely eat all sorts of things. For Paul's Jew and Gentile friends, however, it was a big deal. Paul wanted both groups of Christians to love one another even though their consciences were telling them different things. Paul said, **"As for the one who is weak in faith, welcome him, but not to quarrel over opinions. One person believes he may eat anything, while the weak person eats only vegetables" (Rom. 14:1–2).** Is it a sin to only eat vegetables? Of course not! So, what's the problem?

Some of the Roman Christians thought it was sinful to eat certain foods while other Christians thought it was good to eat them. One person's conscience was bothered while the other person's conscience was not. Paul wants them and us to understand that unless the Bible tells us that something is sinful, we must not spend our time judging or making fun of other Christians for obeying their consciences. Paul makes his point with a big reminder: **"Why do you pass judgment on your brother? Or you, why do you despise your brother? For we will all stand before the judgment seat of God" (Rom. 14:10).** God is the final judge, not us.

Matthew's conscience helped him that day in the tree fort. It was right for him to tell Joseph to stop playing with fire. However, it would not have been good if Matthew made fun of Joseph for wearing a blue shirt. When Christians get together, we must always make sure what our consciences tell us is wrong or sinful is actually wrong or sinful according to the Bible. This will help us to love one another better. Listen to Paul one last time: **"For the kingdom of God is not a matter of eating or drinking but of righteousness and peace and joy in the Holy Spirit"** (Rom 14:17).

Big Idea: Unless something is sinful according to the Bible, we should seek to love other Christians who do things differently than us.

Talk About It: When has your conscience told you something was wrong? Have you ever made fun of someone for doing something differently than you? Why? What are some ways you can seek "peace and joy in the Holy Spirit" with other Christians who are different from you?

Key Verse: *"For the kingdom of God is not a matter of eating or drinking but of righteousness and peace and joy in the Holy Spirit" (Rom. 14:17).*

15

LOVE THEM LIKE JESUS

Have you ever disagreed with someone? Maybe it was a brother or sister, a parent, a friend, or a teacher. Did you stop to think about their point of view or their feelings? If you're like me (a sinner), you probably didn't. Most likely, you felt that your opinion was most important and that you were right. Since the other person was wrong, you were not concerned with how they were feeling. Let's face it, in the moments that we are upset or frustrated, we usually are not the nicest or most compassionate people.

The apostle Paul knows that we need constant reminders and encouragement to love other people the way Christ loves us. In Romans chapter fifteen, Paul gives lots of examples of how Christians should show love to one another. Paul begins with a command that is hard to obey: **"Let each of us please his neighbor for his good, to build him up" (Rom. 15:2).** When people let us down or make us mad, it's hard to think of ways to please *them* instead of ourselves! We want to yell, throw things, or make rude comments. In short, we want to be selfish. That's why we need Paul's next comment so badly: **"For Christ did not please himself, but as it is written, 'The reproaches of those who reproached you fell on me'" (Rom. 15:3).** Paul reaches all the way back to Psalm 69 (the place where "it is written") to make his point: Jesus laid aside his interests and served sinful people who were weak, rude, and undeserving. Compared to what our Lord did, loving our neighbors doesn't seem so impossible!

If you're thinking that this kind of life will take lots and lots of prayer—you're right! After telling us to love our neighbors the way Christ loved us, Paul prays: **"May the God of endurance and encouragement grant you to live in such harmony with one another, in accord with Christ Jesus, that together you may with one voice glorify the God and Father or our Lord Jesus Christ" (Rom. 15:5–6).** Paul knows that God alone is strong enough (after all, he is the King) to cause Christians to live, act, talk, and love like Jesus. Do you struggle to love others when they seem weak, annoying, or frustrating? If so, then you should probably take a lesson from the apostle Paul: *pray.* Ask Almighty God to give you a soft and tender heart that loves Jesus and his people. Sometimes we struggle to love others well because we don't go to God and ask him to help us!

It can be hard to accept other people. It can be really, really hard to accept other people when they make us mad. This is why we need the gospel every day! In the gospel, we are reminded that God loved us when we were unlovable (Rom. 5:6–9). In the gospel, we are reminded that we are accepted into God's family as sons and daughters (Rom.

8:16–17). In the gospel, we are reminded that Christ served people who did not deserve it (Rom. 15:3). The gospel is the reason why Paul says this: **"Therefore welcome one another as Christ has welcomed you, for the glory of God" (Rom. 15:7).** Other people, even other Christians, can be unlovable at times. Think about what Christ has done for you, pray for God's help, then go and love them like Jesus.

Big Idea: Christ's love for us enables us to love others—even when they are unlovable.

Talk About It: What do other people (even other Christians) do to you that makes it difficult for you to love them? Have you ever been tempted to ignore someone or avoid them? Why? How does the gospel help you to love others?

Key Verse: *"Therefore welcome one another as Christ has welcomed you, for the glory of God"* *(Rom. 15:7).*

16

HANG IN THERE!

Do you have any friends or family in another city? Another state? Another country? Another planet? Well, maybe not another planet (I hope), but you probably have written a letter, email, or at least sent a text to friends and family who are distant from you. Did you use their names? Of course, you did! Calling someone by their name is a sign that you know them and care for them. Let's think of it the other way. Have you ever been away from home? Perhaps you left your parents to visit your grandparents or went away to a summer camp. If so, did you want to hear from home? Would it encourage you to receive a letter and see your name written on the envelope? I bet it would. When we want to encourage other people, one of the first things we need to do is call them by name and show them that we care.

The apostle Paul ends his big letter to the Romans by doing exactly that. In chapter sixteen, he calls several of his dear friends by name as a sign that he knows them, loves them, and is concerned about them. Let's see if you can pronounce the names of Paul's friends that are listed in Romans chapter sixteen: Phoebe, Prisca, Aquila, Epaenetus, Mary, Andronicus, Junia, Ampilatus, Urbanus, Stachys, Aristobulus, Herodion, Narcissus, Tryphaena, Tryphosa, Persis, Rufus, Asyncritus, Phlegon, Hermes, Patrobas, Hermas, Philologus, Julia, Nereus, and Olympas.

Wow! Some of those names are hard to say! But imagine you were one of those people. For example, think about Epaenetus. Paul tells us that he was **"the first convert to Christ in Asia" (Rom. 16:5).** This man had a very special relationship with

Paul since he was the first person to repent and believe the gospel in the area of Asia. He would have been an encouragement to Paul and would have also been encouraged to hear that Paul remembers him in his big letter. As a matter of fact, all of the people named in the letter would have felt encouraged to know that the great apostle Paul cared for them. It was not easy (or safe) to be a Christian in Rome at the time that Paul wrote his letter. Hearing your name in Paul's letter would have lifted your spirits like a letter from mom while you're away at summer camp!

Like a good friend, Paul also gives some final warnings for the Christians in Rome. Specifically, he warns them about false teachers (Rom. 16:17). Paul knows that his friends in Rome can be prideful (remember what he said in Romans 12:3), so he warns them about unsaved people who **"by smooth talk and flattery . . . deceive the hearts of the naïve"** **(Rom. 16:18).** Paul knows the only way to protect his Roman friends is to preach the gospel to them over and over: **"Now to him who is able to strengthen you according to my gospel and the preaching of Jesus Christ"** **(Rom. 16:25).** This is what we need too. Christians today, old and young, need to hear the gospel of Jesus Christ every day. The gospel strengthens and guards us so that we, like Paul, treasure Jesus and live our lives in a way that glorifies him. Little Christian, *hang in there*, keep your eyes on Christ, and say, **"to the only wise God be glory forevermore through Jesus Christ! Amen" (Rom. 16:27).**

Big Idea: We need to be encouraged and encourage others to keep looking to Jesus and to live for his glory.

Talk About It: What letter, email, or text encouraged you? Why? Are there Christians living in dangerous places today that you (with your parents' help) could write an encouraging letter to? How does the preaching of the gospel strengthen us?

Key Verse: *"To the only wise God be glory forevermore through Jesus Christ! Amen" (Rom. 16:27).*

"Now to him who is able to strengthen you according to my gospel and the preaching of Jesus Christ, according to the revelation of the mystery that was kept secret for long ages but has now been disclosed and through the prophetic writings has been made known to all nations, according to the command of the eternal God, to bring about the obedience of faith – to the only wise God be glory forevermore through Jesus Christ! Amen" (Rom. 16:25–27).

CPSIA information can be obtained
at www.ICGtesting.com
Printed in the USA
BVHW042237200920
589253BV00002B/7

9 781989 174593